BARNSLEY

THEN & NOW

IN COLOUR

BRIAN ELLIOTT

First published in 2011

The History Press
The Mill, Brimscombe Port
Stroud, Gloucestershire, GL5 2QG
www.thehistorypress.co.uk

British Library Cataloguing in Publication Data.
A catalogue record for this book is available from the British Library.

ISBN 978 0 7524 6402 2

Typesetting and origination by The History Press
Production managed by Jellyfish Print Solutions and manufactured in India

CONTENTS

ACKNOWLEDGEMENTS

Most of the modern images in this book were taken in the spring of 2011 using a Nikon D90 digital camera. It was a task that really did make me appreciate more than ever the skill and ingenuity of Barnsley's photographic pioneers. In more recent years we have been fortunate to have people like Edward Tasker, Sid Jordan and Roy Portman to record our town. This book is dedicated to their memory. My appreciation also goes to Chris and Pearl Sharp at Old Barnsley for their kindness in letting me have access to several of the old photographs in their great collection. In a small way I hope my own work over the years, in the form of photographs, research and writing will also have contributed to this compilation. Finally, thanks are certainly due to Jessica Andrews at The History Press for her encouraging comments and practical advice.

ABOUT THE AUTHOR

Brian Elliott is a former teacher and college manager with a special interest in the history of Barnsley and South Yorkshire. In 1992 he was awarded an M.Phil by the University of Sheffield for his work on Barnsley as a historic market town. He has appeared on BBC Radio Sheffield on many occasions as a local history expert and has made contributions to BBC Radio 4 and BBC and ITV local news programmes, especially on his specialist subject of coalmining history. In recent years Brian has been a volunteer member of the 'Experience Barnsley' Steering Committee, aimed at establishing an innovatory museum and archive centre in the art deco town hall, Barnsley's most iconic public building.

INTRODUCTION

Much of Barnsley has changed beyond recognition since Warner Gothard and his Edwardian photographer colleagues took a series of carefully composed images of the town and district a century or more ago. A great deal disappeared during the interwar period, most notably near the top of Market Hill and along Shambles Street and Church Street. Although much was lost, the new town hall and what was then the Mining and Technical College (now University Campus Barnsley) has enhanced the 'top of town' area, creating a fine civic and campus quarter. Perhaps the greatest change to 'old Barnsley' took place from the 1960s to the 1970s, when many interesting buildings and features in and around the old market disappeared and were replaced by the concrete structures that we see today.

Yet Barnsley is proud of its long history and heritage, founded on the glass, linen and coal industries. 'Experience Barnsley', a new state-of-the-art centre outlining the continuing story of the town and its districts will soon be opening in a revamped town hall after many years of planning. Incorporating archives and study facilities, it should be of interest to people of all ages with Barnsley connections and a tremendous educational asset.

After the 1984–85 miners' strike it was a great struggle for the council, agencies and individuals to restore confidence and regenerate the area. At last, from the early 1990s, strategies began to bear fruit, perhaps no more evident than in and around former pit villages and on old pit sites. Areas such as Grimethorpe and Cortonwood, for example, aided by an infrastructure of new roads and new business locations, have been transformed. The building of the Alhambra Centre was an integral part of the creation of a new Barnsley. In 2003, a thirty-year 'Remaking Barnsley' plan was drawn up to take the town well into the twenty-first century. The first phase, the creation of the Barnsley Transport Interchange, has both brightened and improved communications. Other developments include the Westgate Plaza, Gateway Plaza complex, new Civic Hall and its Creative Design Extension and the Digital Media Centre; plans for a massive demolition and rebuild of the market area are also imminent.

Internationally renowned architect Will Allsop's vision of Barnsley as a Tuscan hill town in the style of Lucca attracted a lot of media attention almost ten years ago, but it started the thought process and now wonderful progress has been made. There's no need for a mile-diameter Allsop halo to be projected from the town hall tower. Anyway, to get to the top of the tower is quite a job – I've tried it.

PINFOLD HILL AND SHAMBLES STREET

PINFOLD HILL AND Pinfold Steps got their names from the small pound used to contain stray farm animals that was once located by the top of the hill overlooking Westgate (Shambles Street), one of the main medieval thoroughfares. Richard Fisher, who somewhat unusually combined alehouse keeping with work as a collier, built his house here *c.*1700. The two little boys in the old photograph on the right make the steps look more interesting, as does the shiny milk churn at the bottom. The whole image was carefully composed by a picture postcard photographer *c.*1905.

WORKMEN ARE FINISHING the landscaping around the old Pinfold Steps and the spectacular modern front of the new Gateway Plaza complex towers over the scene like the stern of a great cruise ship. It is good to see some continuity though: part of the curved frontage of the late eighteenth-century Methodist church (later used as by the Barnsley Boys' Club and now as the Lamproom Theatre) can be seen on the hilltop.

ALHAMBRA

FOR WHOM THE Bell Tolls, starring Gary Cooper and Ingrid Bergman and based on Ernest Hemingway's celebrated novel about the Spanish Civil War, was released in late July 1943. Purpose built as a 2,600-seat theatre in 1915, the Alhambra's flamboyant frontage in white Faena stone made it Barnsley's most spectacular commercial building. It stopped showing films in 1960, a victim of the television age, and became a bingo hall; it was then left forlorn and empty prior to demolition in the late 1980s.

ANYONE WHO HAS not visited Barnsley since 1990 would find it difficult to recognise today's scene. The Alhambra shopping mall has transformed the appearance of Barnsley's townscape, particularly from the eastern Doncaster Road approach. Constructed in 1990–91, the new mall and its five, six and seven storeys of glass, light and dark orange brick and mock-Tudor gabled roofline greet visitors almost like a tall outer bailey, showing Barnsley to be a modern hilltop town. It's good that the Alhambra name has survived, albeit in a modern shopping centre, commemorating a once great place of entertainment during the golden age of the cinema. Not too far away was The Globe, erected at the start of the First World War as a purpose-built 'picture house'. Here, Barnsley people were able to see some of the first silent films. After several years as a live theatre The Globe was demolished during the building of the Western Relief Road in 1990.

MARKET HILL

THERE ARE SEVERAL early views of Market Hill but this one (below), dating from about 1901, is surely one of the best. Just look at the way the patient photographer has encouraged children and local people, even a policeman, to enter the foreground scene. Why? Well, it added interest and sold more postcards. You can just see Aspinall's hat shop, in the lower right of the photograph at the corner of Eldon Street. Just beyond Aspinall's stood one of Barnsley's most noted hostelries: the King's Head Hotel, famous for its formidable lamb roast, the Barnsley chop. At the bottom of the hill stands the Coach and Horses Commercial Hotel, built in 1857 and extending into Peel Street. The properties facing the photographer at the top of the hill disappeared during the interwar clearances, which widened Church Street and created a new civic quarter.

THE TOWN HALL and University Campus Barnsley building now dominate the view up Market Hill. The old King's Head site is occupied by the equally distinctive NatWest bank, and the Eldon Street corner was transformed with the building of the elegant Yorkshire Penny Bank in 1903. Opposite it, the old Coach and Horses Commercial Hotel building remains, but for years it was also used for banking and has been the Yorkshire Bank since 1986. The two-tiered 'plinth' serves as a focal point and resting place for shoppers but remains without any permanent statuary.

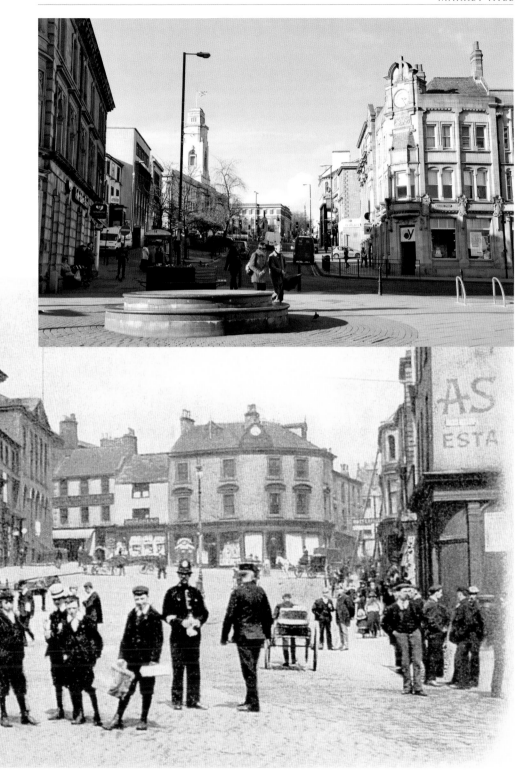

MARKET HILL CONTINUED

MARKET HILL IN the late nineteenth century. The interesting façades of the buildings overlook the broad space where stalls were erected on market days. The frontage of the five-bay King's Head Hotel is a prominent feature, while also in view are part of Butterfield's drapery emporium, a watchmaker's, butcher's, auctioneer's (B. Moss), Guest's grocers and Brady's drapers.

BUTTERFIELD'S (AND MASSIE'S) façade (now Walkabout sports pub) remains instantly recognisable in the modern view. The Arcade, by the side of Guest's old shop, was built *c*.1893. Despite all the changes, the façades of the present-day buildings are in a style that could grace any market town, though some Barnsley people might say that the atmosphere would be much better if market stalls were reinstated on the ancient open space on the hill. Opinions do vary.

THE ROYAL HOTEL/
WHITE BEAR

BARNSLEY'S OLDEST SURVIVING inn was renamed the Royal Hotel following a visit from the Duchess of Kent and Princess Victoria in 1835. The landlady, Mrs Hawksworth, supplied fresh post horses for the royal entourage. The listed Georgian building has had numerous facelifts and further name changes since this photograph was taken in 1981. The sites occupied by adjoining properties

have been used by a variety of high profile businesses since medieval times.

REVERTING TO ITS original name (thank goodness 'Fealty & Firkin' was scrapped) and having been smartened up, the White Bear's attractive appearance is an asset to the town, as is the sympathetically restructured frontage of the adjacent Walkabout Australian bar. The reinstated Venetian Palladian window enhances the view above eye-level and the overall improvement to the former 1980s Thoms store (part of the earlier Butterfield & Massie frontage) is superb. The tall slimline lamp post is also far easier on the eye than its ugly concrete predecessor. It just shows what can be done.

BUTTERFIELD'S

BUTTERFIELD'S WAS PROUD of its No. 1 Church Street address, and its showpiece frontage is illustrated here from an 1891 almanac (right). It was the town's most prestigious drapery store, and stocked a wide range of ladies' and children's fashion goods, from furs, hats and gloves to blouses, dresses and underwear. Butterfield's was also one of the last outlets for the town's premier mill product – fine linen – and some Barnsley people may remember seeing Father Christmas there.

APPROPRIATELY NAMED BUTTERFIELD'S Bar in the late 1990s, Butterfield's has been 'Australianised' in recent years as part of the Walkabout chain of pubs, where (according to its website) it is 'the best place to party in Barnsley'. I'm not sure what Greenwood Butterfield would think about this use of his famous drapery emporium but perhaps he would be relieved that the grand upper façade has been preserved a century or so after his passing.

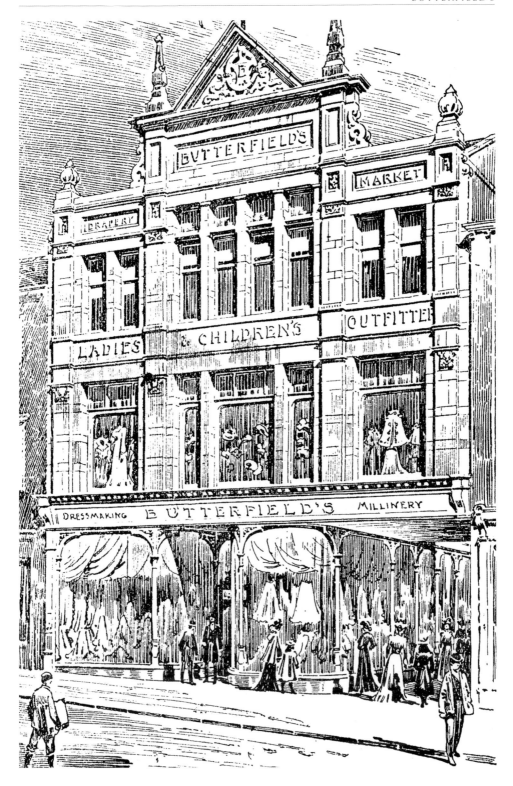

ELSTONE'S

SMALL FAMILY-RUN SHOPS once dominated Barnsley's streets. Henry Elstone's originally opened in 1857, occupying premises at No. 14 Market Hill and a warehouse in George's Yard. Its main business was that of a tobacconist, over the years serving four generations of customers. Latterly it diversified into fine teas, coffees and jams etc. as well as selling newspapers and magazines. In the 1930s photograph we can see the shop manager Mr Brown (left), Miss Ada Humpleby (assistant) and the wholesale manager Harold Farnsworth. The shop soldiered on until closure in 1991.

A BIT OF Milan in Barnsley? Why not. The upper frontage of Pollyanna, Rita Britton's fashion store and café/restaurant now occupies the old Elstone shop, which has an understated exterior that is particularly pleasing to the eye. Upper floors are also used, and some of the best and most avant-garde designers have their products for sale here, attracting custom from far and wide, while the café continues the store's state-of-the-art excellence. A Barnsley lass, Rita started her business in 1967 and it now ranks as the oldest independent fashion outlet in Britain. She was given the honour of Freedom of Barnsley in 2000.

HY. ELSTONE LTD.
Wholesale & Retail
TOBACCONISTS
ABDULLA
CIGARETTES
GOLD FLAKE
"COOLIE" MIXTURE
SUMMIT
THE OLDEST TOBACCON

BARNSLEY WAR MEMORIAL

THE DATE IS Sunday 11 October 1925 and the occasion is the unveiling of the war memorial to commemorate the volunteers ('Barnsley Pals') and many others who lost their lives during what became know as the Great War (right). A large crowd assembled for the formal occasion, and can be seen in the background. It took another seven years for a new town hall to rise from behind the memorial.

BARNSLEY TOWN HALL now forms the backdrop of the war memorial, which is now enclosed by low-profile iron railings. Of course, on Armistice Day and Remembrance Sunday a solemn service commemorating those killed and lost in action is held at the memorial. On 22 June 2010, the 3rd Battalion the Yorkshire Regiment, in desert uniform (having recently returned from Afghanistan), halted here as part of their Freedom Parade through the town.

BARNSLEY TOWN HALL

BARNSLEY'S NEW TOWN hall was officially opened on Thursday 14 December 1933 by HRH Edward Prince of Wales, who ceremonially unlocked the door with a golden key. Alongside, the new Mining and Technical College – an impressive transformation of the west of Church Street – was now complete. The Liverpool architect Arnold Thornely (knighted in 1932) was responsible for both projects. Thornely had recently completed the new parliament building for Northern Ireland at Stormont, Belfast, in Portland stone and in a similar Greek revival style.

TODAY, BARNSLEY TOWN hall is generally regarded as one of the best modern civic buildings in the north of England, particular noted for its art deco features. Shortly after this photograph was taken preparation work began to screen the building prior to a major restoration and the installation of 'Experience Barnsley', a project incorporating heritage objects, interactive themes and archives, scheduled to open in the summer of 2012.

THE MINING COLLEGE/ UNIVERSITY CAMPUS

KING GEORGE VI and Queen Elizabeth leave the new Barnsley Mining and Technical College in October 1937. The building was opened five years earlier when it was described as 'one of the best schools of learning' and 'the largest mining college in the country'. Just visible, standing by the official car is the mayor of Barnsley, Joseph Jones, and the town clerk, Adam Gillfillan.

UNIVERSITY CAMPUS BARNSLEY (previously University Centre Barnsley) is part of the University of Huddersfield, providing higher education opportunities for local people. Despite the state-of-the-art facilities, on entering the welcoming interior there is an overwhelming sense of the building's history. For me, it also brings back memories of sitting my A-levels there, in a hall which I think has now been adapted for media studies work. One day, Barnsley may have its own independent university – you never know.

BARNSLEY COLLEGE

BARNSLEY'S NEW COLLEGE of Technology 'extension' was built *c.*1958–60, on a prime site at the top of Old Mill Lane, facing Church Street. The modernist design by Lyons, Israel and Ellis attracted pleasing comments from the distinguished architectural historian Nikolaus Pevsner when he compiled the West Riding edition of his 'Buildings of England' series of books. The college provided a wide range of vocational courses for many thousands of local people and the opportunity for a second chance to gain general education qualifications.

IN THE SPRING of 2011, Barnsley's newest college building was nearing completion, part of a £60 million regeneration programme. The view looking towards the main Eastgate/Church Street entrance is even more spectacular, with shades of red, green and brown reflecting in the light. The architect appears not to have totally ignored the new building's predecessor: cool, sharp lines contribute to the magnificently modern look.

ST MARY'S CHURCH

THIS MAGNIFICENT LATE nineteenth-century view of St Mary's church is from the Victorian camera of Warner Gothard. The medieval building was remodelled in late Georgian and early Victorian times, most notably by the renowned architect Thomas Rickman, who also got the commission for the new St George's church (see page 36). For centuries, St Mary's had functioned as a 'chapel of ease' for the ancient parish of Silkstone.

THE TREES SURROUNDING St Mary's are now more mature, and although it has lost its Victorian railings, the church continues to look well from Church Street, now sandwiched between University Campus Barnsley and the new Barnsley College building.

PEEL SQUARE

PEEL SQUARE WAS also photographed by Gothard, at a time when horse-drawn cabs were lined up for customers in the middle of the street. The Barnsley Coffee Tavern Company occupied

a suite of upper rooms in the distinctive building facing the cabs, renamed Chronicle Buildings when they were used by the town newspaper. In 1903, motorised taxis first appeared in London and not too long afterwards they also appeared in provincial towns such as Barnsley.

OF ALL THE old Barnsley vistas reproduced in this book, Lowry-like chimneys and people apart, the view looking towards Peel Square has changed the least. The horse-drawn (and even the motor) taxi cabs have long gone of course, but the small white building, Brown's jewellers (and pawnbrokers) remains in business, as does the old Chronicle Buildings, now Chambers' Sports Bar. The now famous plinth has also squeezed into my picture.

TAYLOR'S MILL, PEEL STREET

BARNSLEY'S BIGGEST FACTORY, Taylor's Mill, dominated much of the north side of Peel Street, as can be seen in the nineteenth-century print on the right. The steam-operated mill was opened in 1854 by Edward Taylor, a fourth generation linen entrepreneur, and enlarged over the years. By 1900, surviving Barnsley

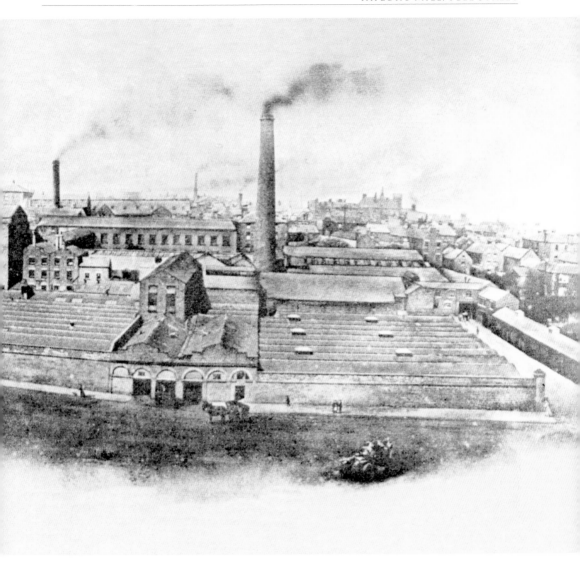

mills concentrated on the luxury market in the wake of the decline of bulk trade. Listed as 'Thomas Taylor & Sons (Barnsley) Ltd' in a 1920 trade directory, the mill then made 'fancy drills, vestings, damask etc.'. It was still a large employer, but its glory days of linen were just about gone. Taylor's functioned until 1931 when the old weaving sheds were taken over by the Yorkshire Tyre Rubber Company. Remnants of the original building remained until the early 1970s.

WOW, WHAT A difference there is in the modern photograph. Shops of the 1960s and 1970s, including a parade set back with what I can only describe as their advertising structures, occupy much of Taylor's old mill frontage today. The modern brick structure in the distance, by Fenton Street, reflects the style of its predecessor, the four- and five-storey mill building that can be seen in the old print, which had been taken over by the William Freeman company.

THE RITZ/PEEL STREET

DO YOU REMEMBER the Ritz? Well, many people do, and with great affection too. It was the poshest cinema for miles around. Purpose built by Union Cinemas in 1937, to the design of Verity and Beverley, it had the plushest of interiors and a Wurlitzer organ whose most famous master was Trevor Willetts. The Ritz's neon-lit art deco façade brought a welcome bit of Hollywood to downtown Barnsley. Talking about 'made in Barnsley', you may have seen the film *Kes* there too.

THE MODERN PHOTOGRAPH shows the same view now: a cleared building site, not long ago occupied by Leo's/Pioneer supermarket. A budget supermarket and its car park will soon rise from this brown field area and the street and townscape of this part of Barnsley will change once again. It has a somewhat unusual name – Lidl, pronounced li-del – and is a German discount chain owned by the giant Schwarz company that operates 7,200 stores worldwide. Better not mention their chief competitor and compatriot, Aldi.

ST GEORGE'S CHURCH

ST GEORGE'S CHURCH, seen here on a picture postcard sent in 1903, dates from 1821 but was enlarged during Victorian times. It was a so-called 'Waterloo' or 'Commissioners'' church, built with money voted by Parliament following a wave of enthusiasm after 1815 to establish new

Anglican places of worship, particularly in burgeoning industrial areas. Thomas Rickman, the Commissioners' lead architect, was the designer, producing what became a landmark building for Barnsley. But his use of iron in the construction, though innovative, contributed to its ultimate demise, as corrosion led to its abandonment and demolition in the late twentieth century.

A NEW ST GEORGE'S church was erected near the top of York Street but it was sad to see the old building fall into disrepair and become the victim of vandalism. Fortunately, the best stained-glass window, based on Pre-Raphaelite Holman Hunt's 'Light of the World' painting (in Keble College, Oxford) was taken out and placed in the new church. The site of the old St George's church is now a garden of remembrance, which still retains the original iron railings, three trees and some monuments. The opened-up view across Pitt Street includes the Gateway Plaza, Westgate Plaza, John Rideal House and Barnsley Town Hall, which all form part of the changing panorama.

PITT STREET METHODIST CHURCH AND TEMPERANCE HALL

DESIGNED BY JAMES Simpson in 1845–46, Pitt Street's Wesleyan church, seen in the photograph on the left next to the Temperance Hall just before demolition in 1984, was a large and imposing late-Classical building. Its façade was a little more restrained than its slightly earlier neighbour, Hindle's Greek-styled Temperance Hall, as it became known. Over the years the Temperance Hall's function has included that of an auction mart, cinema, dancing school, warehouse (Farnsworth's), themed pub (Panama Joe's), gym, Liberal club and offices.

A GREAT GAP now appears where Pitt Street Methodists once attended their large church. The small red-brick building set back from the road with its gable end towards the street was its replacement, but its religious usage did not last long and it became a children's nursery. The old Temperance Hall looks smarter than ever, resplendent in its new livery. It could have looked even better today if the 'TEMPERANCE HALL' lettering had been retained, but this was removed by previous owners.

PITT STREET

PITT STREET WAS one of the most elegant parts of Barnsley. The frontages of the Methodist church and Temperance Hall can clearly be seen on this Edwardian postcard and 'X' marks the entrance of Dr Blackburn's house. The card took nine days to reach the Hudson Terminal in the north-east USA in 1909 (and then found its way back home). Two years earlier the *Lusitania* sailed across the Atlantic in under four days.

IT'S A PITY that so many fine and interesting buildings were demolished along Pitt Street, especially during the 1960s and 1970s. The gaps and the odd unfortunate replacement buildings such as the brick office block just visible beyond the Temperance Hall are far from complementary.

ELDON STREET

AN EARLY VIEW of Eldon Street (right) taken from the bottom of Market Hill a few years before the extension of the Yorkshire Penny Bank, which began in 1914. Notice the large stone-set (cobbled) area in the foreground and the legend 'JOHNSON'S TONICS CURES COUGHS' emblazoned on the gabled frontage of Johnson's chemist's shop at the Eldon Street/ Queen Street corner. Next door was Staples' open-fronted fishmonger's shop. The advertising notice between the two refers to a concert at the Empire. A 'bobby' stands in the road, looking at the photographer, but there is no traffic for him to deal with other than what seems to be a horse and trap.

THE CURVED FRONTAGE of the former Montague Burton building (now used by the

Halifax bank) has been a distinctive feature since the tailoring empire located here in the early 1930s. The restored Yorkshire Building Society building of 1903–14 looks well on the opposite corner. The stone sets have long gone, but the line of the *c.*1840 street remains well defined.

ELDON STREET
CONTINUED

WARNER GOTHARD'S PHOTOGRAPHIC studio can be seen sandwiched between Holdroyd's tailors shop and Swaddle's ironmongers in this rare image of Eldon Street, c.1900. Some of the shops' wares are clearly visible: suit lengths, portrait photographs, saws, tape measures and even bird cages. The ghost-like image in the street is probably of a horse or person moving too fast for the slow shutter speed of the large-frame camera. Notice the typical advertising hoardings in front of a vacant building site and the stylish gas lamp opposite them.

THE GAP WHERE the Victorian hoardings stood was filled in 1909–10 by the stone-fronted façades of the Young Men's Christian Association (YMCA) and Eldon building respectively. The new businesses at street level below include Santander, Quicksilver and NStyle, and Whitegates' estate agents occupy the old Gothard shop, though it had been given a relevant boost when Denton's, another well-known photographic business, took over the premises during the 1950s and early 1960s. Similarly, Swaddle's became T.W. Brown's ironmongery shop from 1908–59.

HARRAL'S

PHOTOGRAPHED BY THE author in 1982, the flamboyant upper façade of Benjamin
Harral's famous jeweller's or 'ring shop' (established 1898) proclaims, in stylish graphics:

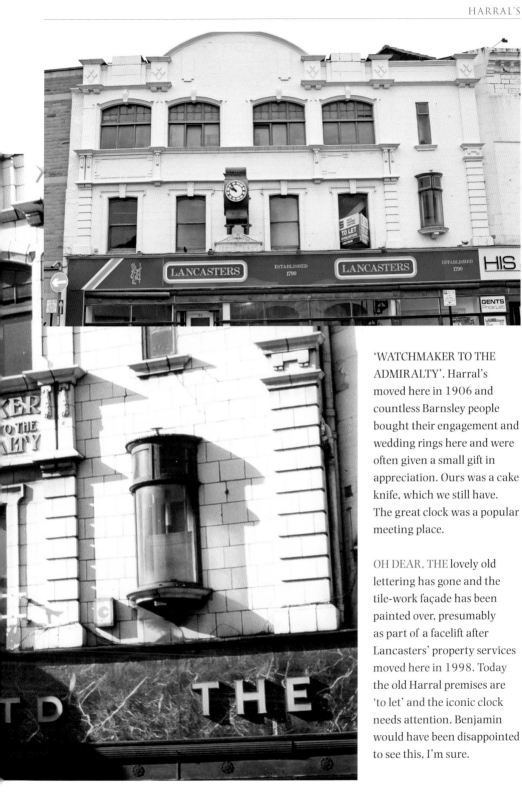

'WATCHMAKER TO THE ADMIRALTY'. Harral's moved here in 1906 and countless Barnsley people bought their engagement and wedding rings here and were often given a small gift in appreciation. Ours was a cake knife, which we still have. The great clock was a popular meeting place.

OH DEAR, THE lovely old lettering has gone and the tile-work façade has been painted over, presumably as part of a facelift after Lancasters' property services moved here in 1998. Today the old Harral premises are 'to let' and the iconic clock needs attention. Benjamin would have been disappointed to see this, I'm sure.

THE CIVIC HALL

A MOBILE TRADER allows his horse to drink from the trough at the junction of Eldon and Kendray Street in this carefully composed view by Warner Gothard, *c.*1895 (right). Across Eldon Street tailor Scholey and Popplewell's 'shaving and hair-cutting saloon' are open for business. The great background building is the Harvey Institute, named in honour of Charles Harvey JP, who gifted the structure to the town twelve years after it had been built by a private company in 1876–77 as the Public and Mechanics' Hall, at a substantial cost of £27,000 (about £1.4 million today).

THE MODERN PHOTOGRAPH shows an even quieter street, although it was taken on a Sunday morning. The trough has long gone but the Civic Hall remains resplendent after its recent major renovation and restoration. It was an expensive project (and went £7 million over budget), exacerbated when engineers found that the Brunel-age builders had not in fact secured the front of the building to the rest of the structure. The central tower has disappeared but the New Civic Hall is surely now one of the most impressive public buildings in the county, with a greatly enhanced interior and providing a variety of exhibitions and events via the new Creative Media Extension and Mandela Gardens at the rear. Barnsley Metropolitan Borough Council deserve credit for what has been achieved here, against all the odds.

KENDRAY STREET

IT CERTAINLY WAS a different world then. The picture below is one of the earliest photographic views of Barnsley, showing Kendray Street and the commemorative fountain at the Eldon Street junction. Robinson's saw mill and a Lowry-like townscape make this an interesting and virtually unrecognisable image for us today. The trough was funded by Mrs Ann Lambert and erected

in memory of her parents, wealthy linen entrepreneurs and well-known benefactors Francis and Ann Kendray. Notice the advertising hoardings beyond Robinson's chimney and the large Quaker Oats poster on the near right of the photograph.

TYPICAL 1970s OFFICE and business-premises architecture, the most dreadful concrete structures imaginable, still occupy this sad-looking area, dating from a ten-year stint when Barnsley was the county headquarters of South Yorkshire County Council. Thank goodness this area will be redeveloped as part of the 'Remaking Barnsley' strategy, along with the provision of a new indoor market. Personally I can't wait.

REGENT STREET

ONE OF MY first photographs of Barnsley, taken in the late 1960s, shows lower Regent Street. Opposite the blackened Queen's Hotel is the almost equally dark courthouse (designed by Reeves in 1861 but converted to a railway station ten years later), then used by Goodworths as a wholesale drapery. The old railway bridge over Eldon Street had recently been demolished and the most striking building, the spired Congregational church of 1856, went the same way in 1971.

THE VIEW TODAY (below left) shows a much cleaner-looking courthouse and Queen's Hotel, the latter recently converted for office accommodation and the former now a well-established bar/pub and art shop. The loss of the spired Congregational church in 1971 and mundane

replacement buildings detract from the former grandeur of one of Barnsley's best Victorian streets. The distinctive Digital Media Centre is just in shot behind the old Courthouse, a contrasting but complementary twenty-first-century building. A grove of traffic lights at this busy junction makes photography difficult but maybe you can spot the Dan Jarvis election poster in a window?

NEW STREET

NEW STREET, ALWAYS busy in Victorian and Edwardian times, contained a variety of small shops and businesses, but at the top (at Island Corner) stood the impressive premises of the Barnsley British Co-operative Society. In the background of the old photograph, left of centre, a sign for Lodge's printer's premises is just visible. Note the large spectacle sign above R.E. Gray's opticians

(No. 7) and next door George Owram functioned as a hatter and hosier. In the nineteenth century one of my maternal great-grandfathers worked in this street as one of Barnsley's numerous boot and shoe makers.

THE YORKSHIRE BANK and Alhambra Centre now occupy the entire south side of New Street but, opposite this, some of the older properties in the earlier photograph have survived. Owram's (No. 5), for example, is now occupied by Gary's Fisheries and Gray's (No. 7) by the Jual 'domestics', an electrical goods shop. It is interesting to see great change alongside some continuity of usage here. Even the block paving mirrors the Edwardian stone-set (cobbled) surface.

QUEEN STREET

THIS EARLY VIEW of Queen Street (right) dates from about 1900 and shows several well-known traders on prime sites, particularly to the left of the photograph. On the right, just in shot, is Benjamin Gaunt's jewellers shop, in business here until 1929. Notice the stone-set street surface. The parked milk cart is an interesting feature, as is the tall attractive gas lamp strategically sited at the edge of May Day Green.

ALTHOUGH THE MODERN view below is taken from a wider angle, the stone-fronted building on the left is still recognisable. Gaunt's jeweller's is now occupied by two well-known brands – Thornton's and

H. Samuel – and the tall horizontal panelling at the front of the former Woolworth's building overlooks the pleasantly pedestrianised scene.

QUEEN STREET
CONTINUED

QUEEN STREET, LOOKING towards May Day Green on a sunny day in the late 1930s. Burton the tailor's is the most prominent building occupying the corner, next to it is the Three Cranes Hotel.

QUEEN STREET, BARNSLEY.

Across the road is another 1930s introduction: Marks & Spencer.

THE OLD THREE Cranes Hotel with its pediments has been replaced by early 1970s Woolworths' architecture on the left side of the photograph; the ancient May Day market area was redeveloped about the same time. The entrance to Queen Street from Peel Square and Market Hill, however, is relatively unchanged in appearance. The attractive stone building on the right, now occupied in part by Santander, was rebuilt in an identical style to its predecessor, even down to replacing the Palladian window and archway, which just shows what can be done.

CHEAPSIDE

AN EARLY YORKSHIRE traction omnibus makes its way along Cheapside on a market day in
1920s Barnsley. The pavements are crowded outside Thorpe's Dress and Drapery Warehouse and
Albert Hirst's butcher's shop. Across the road is Blakey's wallpaper shop and, just in view, the
corner of the Public Benefit Footwear store.

IT'S PRETTY HARD to replicate the same scene today, but if you stand with your back to the main entrance to the Alhambra Centre, this is the view (above). Architecture from the 1970s predominates what used to be an interesting scene, but at least people can walk and talk with relative ease. The indoor market on the right is due to be developed, and hopefully fairly soon.

MAY DAY GREEN

MAY DAY GREEN and its open-air market are an increasingly distant memory. The photograph on the right was taken in 1969 when Barnsley was celebrating its borough centenary, hence the bunting and elevated coat of arms. Bull and bear baiting and rousing meetings of artisans and miners once took place in this ancient open space area.

LOOKING ACROSS WHAT was the old May Day Green market today, the kiosk perhaps offers a symbolic nod towards the old market but, background buildings apart, you could not have a more contrasting scene. It's good when the place 'comes to life' with temporary stalls on special occasions.

FISH MARKET

MANY BARNSLEY PEOPLE will remember the old Kendray Street market, its fish sellers in particular. The sights, sounds and smells from such places linger in the memory. There were a variety of other stalls there on market days, including one chap who sold wonderful hot roast pork

sandwiches – unbeatable. This lovely photograph was taken by V. C. Silverwood in 1974 and has a timeless quality, although I'm not too sure about the 1970s fashions.

MAY DAY GREEN, as it is known today, but this is really the site of part of the old Kendray Street fish market. These ribbed prefabricated concrete façades and uniform business units stand mostly empty, but are creatively used via the 'Art in the Precinct' scheme. The sights, sounds and smells of the market disappeared when these properties were erected during the early 1970s. The three-storey, three-bay Cross Keys Hotel and the market Weigh House more or less stood where the modern Santander and Ilkeston Travel premises are now located.

CANNON HALL

THIS LATE NINETEENTH-CENTURY image of Cannon Hall is another captured by Warner Gothard. It appears to have been a quiet winter or spring day, with no one in the picture. But Cannon Hall was still a family home in those days, occupied by the Spencer-Stanhopes. Their enterprising forebears, the Spencers, had established a fine country house here during the eighteenth century, designed by John Carr, one of the North's most celebrated architects. The lovely park was landscaped by Richard Woods who also worked at Cusworth Hall near Doncaster.

ALTHOUGH MID WEEK in our modern photograph, small groups of people enjoy the spring sunshine in front of the house, relaxing on one of the benches or on the grass. In the foreground several dog walkers had just passed by. In the care of Barnsley Council since 1951, and supported in recent years by its Friends' group, Cannon Hall Museum and Country Park has become one of the most popular attractions for visitors to South and West Yorkshire; and being a short distance away from Barnsley, the picturesque village and parkland provides local people with a wonderful place for a walk in some of the best countryside you will see anywhere. The scene has changed relatively little since Gothard's era, and perhaps looks even more attractive today.

WENTWORTH CASTLE

THE MAGNIFICENT PALLADIAN and Baroque wings of Wentworth Castle, when it was still the home of Captain Bruce Wentworth, were also photographed by Gothard in about 1890. The Captain was in the process of establishing a large collection of rhododendrons in the garden and grounds and roaming highland cattle add interest at the front of the house. Formerly known as Stainborough Hall, the name change was part of the ongoing eighteenth-century rivalry between the Wentworths here and their illustrious cousins 8 miles away at Wentworth Woodhouse.

IN RECENT YEARS, the Wentworth Castle and Stainborough Park Heritage Trust (and its partners), inspired by BBC2's 2003 *Restoration* programme, has, thanks to successful funding bids, carried out a phased amount of restoration and development of the historic park's buildings, grounds and monuments, including the first earl of Strafford's mock castle, once more a romantic folly to explore and enjoy. A Parkland Trail has been established and both red and fallow deer graze in the Grade I listed landscape. The badly-needed restoration of the Victorian Conservatory is the next funding, restoration and conservation challenge. The castle itself remains home to the Northern College of Adult Residential Education but there are plans for the Trust to open up the main building to the public through guided tours. From April through September the gardens and parkland are open, along with the visitor centre. There are also special events.

BARNSLEY HIGH SCHOOL
FOR GIRLS

LAMB, OF RACECOMMON Road, produced a series of quality postcards of local buildings, people and scenes during the Edwardian era. This example shows Barnsley High School for Girls shortly after its opening on the new Hall Balk Lane site in 1909. Founded in 1905, it had previously functioned from the Conservative Club in town. Architecturally, it is one of Barnsley's most impressive larger buildings. The first headmistress was the apparently formidable Miss A. J. Robinson, appointed on a modest salary of £300 a year (about £17,000 today). She presided over 167 girls, sixty of whom were student teachers and over the years the school developed an excellent reputation.

THE WROUGHT-IRON GATES commemorating the fiftieth anniversary of the old school (1905–55) are still intact but it only functioned as a girls' school for another eighteen years: it was re-named Hall Balk School in 1973 and had become fully comprehensive by 1977. In the 1980s it had a short life as a sixth form college before eventually becoming part of Barnsley College. In recent years the building and grounds were sold for private housing development and the school was converted into apartments. Today, the exterior of the building looks little different to its appearance in Lamb's superb Edwardian photograph.

RACE STREET
SWIMMING BATHS AND
THE METRODOME

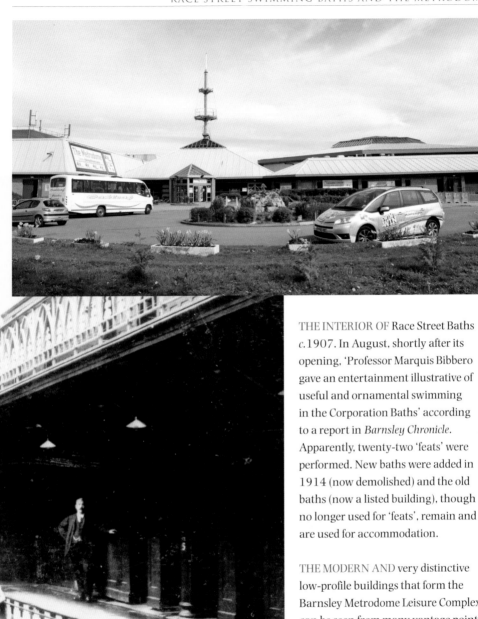

THE INTERIOR OF Race Street Baths
c.1907. In August, shortly after its
opening, 'Professor Marquis Bibbero
gave an entertainment illustrative of
useful and ornamental swimming
in the Corporation Baths' according
to a report in Barnsley Chronicle.
Apparently, twenty-two 'feats' were
performed. New baths were added in
1914 (now demolished) and the old
baths (now a listed building), though
no longer used for 'feats', remain and
are used for accommodation.

THE MODERN AND very distinctive
low-profile buildings that form the
Barnsley Metrodome Leisure Complex
can be seen from many vantage points
due to their hilltop setting overlooking
Oakwell, Barnsley Football Club's
ground. Swimming and leisure
facilities include the Space Adventure
water attraction featuring the 'Space
Bullet' water slide. The Metrodome is
managed and operated by Barnsley
Premier Leisure (BPL).

THE BUS STATION/
TRANSPORT INTERCHANGE

BARNSLEY'S BUS STATION opened for the first time on 13 December 1938. Over the years it has experienced several revamps but many people remember the central platform and threepenny-bit kiosk (Haigh's) with affection and as convenient meeting point. This view dates from the mid 1960s, as a conductress makes her way to the Yorkshire Traction offices. In the distance, the large Ceag building can be seen, where bulbs and lamps for the coalmining industry were manufactured.

BARNSLEY NO LONGER has a 'bus station' but a gleaming Transport Interchange, completed in 2007 after a two-year, £24.5 million build; the first main phase of the thirty-year 'Remaking Barnsley' scheme, it was designed by the Manchester-based architects Jefferson Sheard. Barcelona in Barnsley? Well, the vibrant Mediterranean colours and sensuous curves of the entrances and exits brighten up the views from lower Regent Street, Eldon Street and elsewhere. One of five other South Yorkshire examples, it has the most striking appearance of them all.

LOCKE PARK TEAROOM

SMART-LOOKING STAFF outside Locke Park tearooms photographed shortly after its grand opening in 1911. The council had struggled to find the £510 (almost £30,000 in today's money) building costs, but the facility proved to be very popular, especially on Sundays, gala days and throughout the summer months.

OVER THE YEARS the café has suffered from vandalism and maintenance requirements but it is good to see it functioning again. The Friends of Locke Park have worked very hard to raise considerable funding for the building. Good public parks always have somewhere for refreshments so the Friends' campaigns and efforts have been very worthwhile.

LOCKE PARK BANDSTAND

BRASS BANDS WERE in such great demand that bandstands were included in the sales catalogues of iron foundries. The Locke Park bandstand was made by the Lion Foundry company of Kirkintilloch, Scotland, at a cost of £236 (about £13,500 today). The official opening in 1908 attracted a huge park crowd of about 25,000. The popularity of Sunday afternoon concerts is also evident in this picture postcard, though the grass appears to be in need of mowing.

TODAY THE BANDSTAND remains an attractive feature, still intact after more than a century. Look carefully and you will see, however, that some minor ornate features have gone, and part of the structure has been painted in bright colours, while the Locke Park tower is now obscured by mature trees on the skyline. The graffiti-clad container to the right of the photograph is hopefully a temporary placement. Oh, and the grass has been cut.

JOSEPH LOCKE AND DICKIE BIRD

PAID FOR WITH subscriptions, the Institute of Civil Engineers commissioned the Italian sculptor Baron Marachetti to create a bronze figure of Joseph Locke, their former president, and asked that it be placed beside those of Stephenson and Brunel in St Margaret's Garden, Westminster. The request was refused, but on 10 January 1866 the statue was unveiled near the main entrance of Locke Park. Barnsley's most famous son (Locke had spent his childhood here) had come home and

his stone image was featured in many Edwardian picture postcards, though none as delightful as this example on the left.

THAT'S OUT! HAROLD 'Dickie' Bird, Barnsley's world-famous cricket umpire at the unveiling ceremony of his statue, June 2009. The life-size bronze was the creation of another celebrated Barnsley character, the sculptor Graham Ibbeson. The site chosen, near St Mary's church, is just a few yards from the spot where Dickie was born. The statue is now probably Barnsley's most famous tourist attraction, and is certainly a real eye-catcher for passing traffic.

ROY MASON MP
AND DAN JAMES MP

BARNSLEY'S NEWLY ELECTED MP, the former coalminer Roy Mason (b.1924), photographed on the House of Commons members' terrace in 1953 (left). Mason went on to achieve high office in the Wilson and Callaghan governments, most notably as Secretary of State for Defence and Secretary of State for Northern Ireland. He remains the town's most distinguished politician, active in the Commons and Lords (as Lord Mason) from the administrations of Churchill and Attlee to the Blair and Brown eras.

LIKE ROY MASON, Dan Jarvis, pictured here outside Westminster (right), entered Parliament through a by-election, on 3 March 2011. Formerly a Parachute Regiment officer, Dan's military career has included two deployments to Afghanistan, initially as part of a vital reconnaissance team in Helmand Province and more recently as a company commander in the Special Forces Support Group. The Barnsley Central MP has quickly made his mark in both his constituency work and in Parliament, a fresh and energetic representative for the people and town.

GRAHAM'S ORCHARD

LOOKING DOWN GRAHAM'S Orchard in the direction of Peel Square on a winter's day (right). This atmospheric scene was captured by local photographer Sid Jordan in about 1957 (the print was given to me by Roy Portman) but the stone-set street surface is a relic of a much earlier Barnsley. John Graham once occupied a property near the top of the hill here, by the Wellington (and later Lord Nelson) public house. The sign of the Temple of Muses pub can be seen on the left of the photograph and the premises of G. Partridge, plumbing and heating engineer, on the right.

SID JORDAN'S DRAMATIC picture couldn't be matched today. Several buildings, particularly on the right side of today's view, have gone and the attractive street surface appears to be covered with patched tarmac. The double-yellow lines don't help appearances. Brownes Bar and the relatively new (2006) Joseph Bramah pub are the buildings on the left of the street. It is good that Wetherspoon's have named their pub after the locally-born engineer whose prolific and diverse inventions include what became universally known as the Bramah Lock.

MINERS' INN, 'HONEST DODWORTH'

THE COSTUMES AND musicians may look extraordinary but this assembly of 'honest Dodworthers' outside the Miners' Inn was to celebrate the coronation of George V on Thursday 22 June 1911 (left). No doubt the occasion was a boost for landlord Richard Dixon's trade. Note the Ambulance Station sign under the inn name. The dangers of Dodworth pit, where my paternal grandfather worked, were never far away.

STAN EGLEY AND Richard Robinson, two modern Dodworth-born men, stand outside what used to be the Miners' Inn (above). After closure the building was adapted for usage as a children's nursery (Noah's Ark Kindergarten) but now functions as Noah's Ark Fancy Dress shop, maybe very appropriate in view of the costumes in the old photograph.

OLD WHITE BEAR INN, SHAMBLES STREET

THE SOUTH YORKSHIRE Miners' Association (an early trade union for mineworkers) was formed in 1858 when sixty-two men from twenty-six pits met at the Old White Bear Inn, Shambles Street. In this *c.*1890 image (right) it appears that the landlord, William Goodworth, and his family are at the doorway looking at the photographer. Mrs Goodworth's body language suggests that she had had enough of all the posing. The Methodist pioneer John Wesley preached from the steps at the rear of the inn in 1786 and concluded in his journal, 'Surely God will have a people in this place.'

TODAY, THE MID-1970s Barnsley Central Library is the dominating building on the upper north side of Shambles Street. The medieval Old White Bear and other inns were cleared by the late 1930s. The ceramic heritage panels facing the main road include the spines of books by local authors. 'Shambles' is a common town name, taken from the butcher's stalls that once occupied part of the street frontage, especially on market days, but 'Westgate' was the ancient name for this busy thoroughfare.

MINERS' HEADQUARTERS

THE DISTINCTIVE-LOOKING YORKSHIRE miners' office cost a relatively modest £8,000 (£365,600 today) to build. Once completed in 1874, it became probably the first purpose-built trade union headquarters in the world. Its secretary John Normansall referred to its 'cheerful and pleasant appearance' though he rightly reminded those attending its official opening of the dreadful conditions of work that miners experienced daily. The Mence obelisk (demolished in 1931) at the

top of Old Mill Lane was a popular resting and meeting place, as can be seen in this Edwardian view (left). Note the fashionable lady walking towards the photographer, down one of Barnsley's more elegant streets: Huddersfield Road.

STREET FURNITURE, TRAFFIC and road markings apart, this scene above has changed little since Edwardian times although the obelisk at the top of Old Mill Lane has long gone. The miners' offices now serve as the national headquarters of the National Union of Miners (NUM). During the 1984–85 miners' strike the building was sometimes referred to as 'Arthur's Castle' after Arthur Scargill, the miners' leader. An annual lecture is still held in the magnificent Miners' Hall here and wreaths (just visible in this photograph) are ceremoniously laid in front of the Graham Ibbeson miners' memorial statue, lest we forget.

BARROW PIT DISASTER

WARNER GOTHARD'S MONTAGE postcard commemorated the horrific cage disaster at Barrow Colliery, Worsbrough, on Friday 15 November 1907. Seven men were hurled to their deaths. Their portraits are illustrated on the card below. One young miner rushed to the cabin where the bodies were laid and asked to check their identities. Kneeling, he soon burst into tears after recognising the battered face of his best mate.

TO COMMEMORATE THE centenary of the Barrow pit disaster a tree-planting ceremony and plaque unveiling took place at Birdwell in January 2007, with the mayor of Barnsley, Councillor Len Picken,

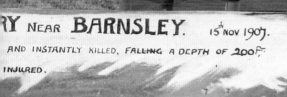

officiating. The magnificent Barrow Branch banner also made what is nowadays a rare public appearance on this special occasion.

CORTONWOOD

LOOKING TOWARDS CORTONWOOD Colliery, this is a photograph taken by the well-known South Elmsall picketer Arthur Wakefield during the 1984–85 miners' strike (left). The announcement of the pit's closure was the spark that ignited the start of the year-long dispute. Cortonwood finally closed at the end of October 1985, and its buildings were hastily obliterated; the shafts were capped four years later, 113 years after they had been sunk with remarkable skill and so much optimism.

ALTHOUGH NOT TAKEN from exactly the same spot, part of the old, now landscaped Cortonwood Colliery muck stack can be seen in the background of the modern photograph above. The site was originally transformed into a retail park by St Paul's Developments during the late 1990s, but the old pit site is now occupied by Morrison's supermarket and McDonald's restaurant as well as a variety of other stores, business offices and houses, all served by the Dearne Towns Link Road. 'The Alamo', the iconic picketers' hut, stood at the Brampton end of the lane leading to the colliery during the 1984–85 miners' strike.

Other titles published by The History Press

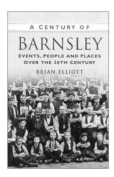

A Century of Barnsley

BRIAN ELLIOTT

This book provides a striking account of the changes that have so altered Barnsley's appearance and records the process of transformation. Drawing on detailed local knowledge of the community, and illustrated with a wealth of photographs, this book recalls what Barnsley has lost in terms of buildings, traditions and ways of life. It also acknowledges the regeneration that has taken place and celebrates the character and energy of local people as they move through the first years of this new century.

978 0 7509 4903 3

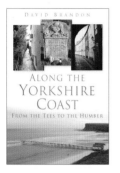

Along the Yorkshire Coast

DAVID BRANDON

This book is a unique record of a journey along the beautiful and often dramatic Yorkshire coastline, tracing the region's diverse industry, the history of its settlements, seaside resorts and fishing quays, and reflecting upon the different uses to which man has put the resources where sea and land meet. With a blend of photographs, fact, folklore and social history, David Brandon offers a fascinating and evocative look the county's local history, and should capture the imagination of anyone who knows the places that are featured.

978 0 7524 5732 1

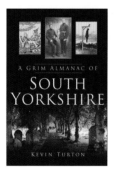

A Grim Almanac of South Yorkshire

KEVIN TURTON

A Grim Almanac of South Yorkshire is a collection of stories from the county's past, some bizarre, some fascinating, some macabre, but all equally absorbing. Revealed here are the dark corners of the county, where witches, body snatchers, highwaymen and murderers have stalked. Accompanying this cast of gruesome characters are old superstitions, omens, strange beliefs and long-forgotten remedies for all manner of ailments.

978 0 7524 5678 2

The Little Book of Yorkshire

GEOFFREY HOWSE

The Little Book of Yorkshire is a fascinating, fact-packed compendium of the sort of information which no-one will want to be without. The county's most eccentric inhabitants, famous sons and daughters, royal connections and literally hundreds of intriguing facts about Yorkshire's landscape, cities, towns and villages come together to make one handy, pocket-sized treasure trove of trivia. Soak up the vast array of quirky tales in this remarkably engaging little book, this is essential reading for visitors and locals alike.

978 0 7524 5773 4

Visit our website and discover thousands of other History Press books.

www.thehistorypress.co.uk